APHRODITE'S ANORAK

Aphrodite's Anorak

HUGH McMILLAN

PETERLOO POETS

First published in 1996
by Peterloo Poets
2 Kelly Gardens, Calstock, Cornwall PL18 9SA, U.K.

A catalogue record for this book is available
from the British Library

ISBN 1-871471-58-3

Printed in Great Britain by
Latimer Trend & Company Ltd, Plymouth

ACKNOWLEDGEMENTS: Some of these poems were first published in *Chapman, Cencrastus, The London Magazone, The Listener, The Spectator, Poetry Review, The Scotsman, Poetry Ireland, Cyphers, Skinkling Star, Lines Review, New Writing Scotland, Poetry Australia, Spectrum* and in the publications *Triumph of the Air* (Envoi Press, 1988), *Tramontana* (Dog and Bone, Glasgow, 1990), *Horridge* (Hugh Who? Press, Dumfries, 1993) and *Horridge* (Chapman, Edinburgh, 1994).

Almost a Scottish Haiku

Here's tae us, wha's
Like us? Dam' few an' they're a'
on tea towels.

Contents

Page

9 The World Book of the McMillans
10 A Present of a Submarine
11 A Very Small Miracle
12 Leaving Scotland by Train
13 The Spanish Soldier
15 Anglophobia
17 May Revision
19 War Games Night
20 Willie
21 Dundee Jute Mill, Turn of the Century
22 Monday Midnight
23 People Were Late for Your Party
24 VE Day: Hexham
25 A Leaving
26 Dear Sammy
28 On the Retirement of Mr. D. Douglas
29 Nebelgard Girl
30 Graeco-Roman Culture
31 Tucker, as Always
32 Saturday 21st May
33 The X Files: Bonnybridge, October '95
34 What You Feel Before You Get Eaten by a Bear
35 Hans from Wuppertal
36 Reflections on the Aphrodite of Rhodes
37 History at Knossos
38 The Stone Princess
39 Vlad the Inhaler
40 Targets
41 Aine
42 Address to a Galway Pen
43 Easdale

44 Getting too Late for Football
45 Blethers
46 On the Hoof
47 Obersalzberg
48 Sports Day
49 Louisana Train
50 Letter from the 24th Congress of the Communist Party
51 History
53 At the Swings
54 Surprise Attacks
55 Bus Station
56 The Zoo
57 Rumours
58 Angles
59 Shug, Alex, Jock, Willie ...
60 Lynn Wilson Says a Prayer for Robert Burns
61 The Little Summer of San Demetrios
62 The Cargo of the 'Hopeful Binning of Bo'ness', Bound for the
    Darien Peninsula, 1699
63 As We Go Home
64 In Search of Leanne
65 Hole in the Wa' — April '96
67 Saturday Afternoon in the Grotto
68 Happy New Year

The World Book of the McMillans

Dear **Hugh McMillan**,
you have been selected by our clan computer
to receive a copy of
The World Book of the McMillans $149.95
(including unique hand painted coat of arms).
Have you ever considered, **Hugh McMillan**,
your family ties and heritage?
In these pages, **Hugh**,
you will bear witness to the heroism
and industriousness of your ancestors
and learn about the forbears
who shaped the history of the world,
like **Fergus McMillan, the 8th Man of Moidart,**
Hector 'Steamboats' McMillan,
the inventor of the 12 Bore Scrotal Pump Beam,
Brian 'Big Shuggie' McMillan, Golf Caddie to the Stars,
and many many others,
though probably not **Archie McMillan**
who died of silicosis
or **James and Colin** who drowned in the Minch,
or **Struan** who drank himself to death
in that corner of the Central Bar.
To bear witness to that kind of thing,
Hugh McMillan,
it costs a bit more.

A Present of a Submarine

The day I got it
I was in a lay-by,
a knuckle of tar near Lugar,
and the sun against the green slopes
of farms was yellow like butter.
I was on the back seat and the submarine,
black, with working parts, from the
poshest shop in Edinburgh, was on
my knees. I remember an open
window, blisters of heat on the dimpled
upholstery and sweat on my neck
and legs.
He said it was only a joke
and she said not the type of joke
I ever want to hear
and then there was no more wash
of cars or birdcalls but silence
like a choir in my head.

I fingered the long snout of
the submarine, the conning tower,
the propellors that moved,
the lines sleek as fish.
That's it, it might as well be it
he said, and the door slammed,
and he strode into the grass like
a god decked in light
and when he swept his hand
in a final cutting motion down
I shook and let go of the cruel
prow at last
for the safety of tears.

A Very Small Miracle

A lamb was born near Dunnet Head,
tumbling in a yellow broth of legs
on the dark earth,
finding its feet just before
the brawling wind from the skerries did.

Nobody paid much heed.
The ewes were not easily impressed
by gyniatrics, and two old women
talked on about tomatoes.
There wasn't even a farmer there
to count this a triumph for finance.

The dreaming lamb wobbled
on the lip of cold reality.
At thirty seconds old it had felt
the first rough edge of a tongue
and already knew that life
was not a bed of turnips.

At a minute
it was standing quite still
staring rudely at me,
as if it knew that being born
a sheep here,
in these extremes of circumstance,
was a very small miracle indeed.

Leaving Scotland by Train

It's not easy.
Near Perth there's a conspiracy
of gravity and guilt
that propels me forward in my seat
to squint at my motherland
from a foetal position,
my nose snorkelling through the coffee
and the world whirling backwards,
disappearing gaily down some Scottish plughole,
an Omphalos near Denny
where the land is conjured back
with all the sheep and the seagulls and the trees
still buttoned on it,
and broken down to formless green.

I daren't open my eyes
in case it's really done the trick
and I'm bobbing like a peeled lychee
in the gynaecological soup,
a heart pulsing in my ear
and a gentle voice saying:
"Where do you think you're going, you bastard?
Stay here. Where it's warm."

The Spanish Soldier

Andrew has just come in, flashing us
an easy smile, the way he does when
he's got a half eaten earthworm
in his fist or is wearing
the chicken as an overshoe.
This time he's carrying a
small figure he's unearthed upstairs.

The Spanish soldier has a fawn
uniform and forage cap. One of his arms
is severed at the elbow and he leans
cheerfully as if the missing hand
had once carried a suitcase of lingerie,
or good paperbacks, or a few
things packed for a High Life Break
in Rimini. His face, once tanned,
is chipped but it still radiates
a boisterous bonhomie.

I had a whole collection once,
mostly square jawed American types
with bazookas in their teeth.
They were a perfect fighting force,
ready at any moment
to turn on the cat, the neighbours,
each other, unburdened by any strand
of conscience.
All except the Spanish soldier.
Rifle slung, knees casually bent,
a smile playing on his lips,
he never fitted in.
He couldn't fire his gun unless
you held him off the ground
and he was just too bloody affable.
He spread disaffection in the ranks;

a wordless plastic form of pacifism.
We tried execution once, for cowardice,
but the Spanish soldier was made
of something very hard and wouldn't
break.

I thought he'd finally bought it
in '69 with all the rest,
when we used home made napalm
in the paddy field that was my garden.
Where's he been since then?
Some Peace Studies Seminar at Bradford
University, perhaps, or Berkely,
California. Somewhere hot,
for his stoop is even more pronounced
and his leg has slightly warped.

Andrew's grinning.
He thinks he's found a new recruit
but I can tell, even now,
from the confidential way he's
bending over Darth Vader,
that the Spanish soldier has not,
in any sense,
lost his inclination to the left.

Anglophobia

Sometimes, after ten pints of Pale in Mather's,
my pals and I discuss, with reasoned calm,
the origins of Anglophobia.

The philosophy was mother's milk to me.
Our cat was called Moggy the Bruce.
In 1966 my uncle Billy died on his knees
before the telly screaming "It didnae
cross the line ye blind bastard!"
I remember my Grandad, seventy five
and ridged with nicotine, sitting, grimly watching
a schoolgirls' hockey match. Hands like shovels,
he'd never even seen a game with sticks
but he was bawling "Bully up, Fiji,
get intae these English!"

An expression of lost identity, they say.
Some identity.
We were the most manic crew of cut-throats
out, never happy unless we were fighting,
preferably each other; any venue,
Turkestan to Guadelope.
It was only after the Pax Britannica
that any of us had a free minute between rounds
to contribute to the culture of the world.

By some strange alchemy we had however found
the untapped source of arrogance and up
to our arses in mud we could thumb our noses
at the Florentines and all the other poofs
of the Renaissance and take some solace
from thumpings by our betters by claiming
moral victory; a piece of turf from Solway
Moss and the crossbar from Culloden.

But despite all that, and sober, the limp
red lions stir the blood and in a crowd of
fellow ba-heids I'll conjure up the pantheon
of Scotland's past and jewel it with lies.
Unswerving stubborness.
I suppose that in the graveyard of nations
Scotland's epitaph will not be a volume
like the French but a single line:
"Ye'll be hearing from us."

May Revision

Answers. Remember there are three,
one each from Sections A and B
and one from those or Section C,
though that one could be
hard I reckon.
May Revision,
the long days beckon.

Write lucidly, remember.
Fill the page.
Be sure to know where
dates apply. Gauge
the time. You know the drill,
and can see the sun
spark clouds of broom on dreaming hills.

Remember Sarajevo. Who can say
the province that it sat in,
the time of murder, month and day,
and the name of the assassin?
Alison, you know better than to chatter
and stray to thoughts of love,
or sex, and things that really matter.

Hard work, remember.
That's the way you all succeed.
Don't you dare relax,
or heed
friends that do. And class,
don't dance on old chalk paths
or run stark naked through the grass.

Remember this, one last good luck.
Take two pens
and if you're stuck
move on. And if you've sense
move on, forget the lot.
Do your May Revision
in an older school of thought.

War Games Night

Belgium, where in hell is that?
says the Czar, big Dan Gibson, as he moves,
knee deep in cardboard troopers, from
the Steppes. The Kaiser, a can of lager in his
hand, laughs and with an old ruler
moves files of Uhlans across the Lys.

Big Dan has little knowledge of the land
or the intricacies of the Schlieffen Plan.
He makes the conscripts walk in bare feet
from the Ukraine. He's lost in the field kitchens
in Crimea. The artillery's in Vladivostock
while the gunners lounge about Kiev.

His peasants advance down the barrels of
the German guns and are reduced to pulp.
Little piles of counters join the fag ash
and the empty bottles round the map.
Got you there you old bastard, the Kaiser
jokes, and big Dan shrugs.

Albert of the Belgians is at the bog and
Ludendorff is making toast. Only Dan is
at the board. Crowned in white smoke he is still
facing west. A million men, I hear
him muse, well well.

Through the window an August breeze moves
the distant skeletons of trees
and I am tempted to think of endless blood
on the Vistula when the likes of big Dan smile.

Willie

"Drunk or sober,
yon man can pit a carpet boul
or a keystane right oan the button."
Willie is nodding modestly
in the Fleshers' Arms,
70 proof, if he's a day.

Willie doesn't age.
Like his dykes he weathers.
He hasn't lost his hair,
but mislaid it in an absent way:
it's strung up there somewhere
on the rich topography of scalp
as thick as ever
but vitrified,
as impenetrable as his handiwork.

Below it, creases run
through the skin
like dry river beds.
There are hard callouses
round the smile
that defines and defies his history.

His face is a map
and like all landscapes
is variable.
Willie hasn't always been good.
I think he predates such concepts.
He is both sides of a very old coin.
The man *is* Galloway.

Dundee Jute Mill, Turn of the Century

They stand crucified by loom ribs and spindles,
these hemp women made from shadow,
with their skull heads doubled over machines
that worked, but not for them.
They present their misery unabashed,
unwilling to hide it,
unable even to conjure, for a shutter second, smiles.

In the foreground there is a youth.
He is small
(The nearest women are bending to his height)
but there is more than a hint of swagger
in the watch chain,
the slightly bending knee,
the hand laid proprietorially on a spool of cloth.
He is a golden boy:
he shines even in this glory of sepia.

It is the way the world is:
and you know the women will die
near the looms,
their certainties the more enduring,
and that the boy's chest will be torn
by machine guns,
all the puff and pride blown to smoke forever.
He will not live to see the skeleton of his mill
or hear the women, weeping still.

Monday Midnight

Through the window
the houses shift; a dreamy selentropy.
Stairs hung with creepers vanish
in starlight and smudge.
The night is heavy,
the birds and I squeal beneath it.

Just then I imagined you were laughing
and, for once, it was like knives.

In a little puddle of light,
surrounded by the boxes
you brought ashore like from a shipwreck,
still unpacked,
I sit and I dream
of syssarcosis.

People Were Late for Your Party

A castle embedded in November.
In the firelight and the snap of candles
you sit frowning, working up a temper.
"Typical" you say, "it's all a shambles"
and you shake your long hair and pace the floor
with your dress silently sweeping shadows
and when you bend over the fire once more
your face is changed to seamed white stone; it glows.
As wind buckles windows, howls down the flue
and the rain spits on burning logs like rind
I stand and wonder at the debt that's due
and gracefully for all these years declined.
"Won't all this be spoiled if they don't come, Hugh?"
but nothing will be spoiled unless they do.

VE Day: Hexham

The brassy music floats
down quintessential streets,
past stones cicatrized by histories
and now, by bunting.
On flickering televisions
coralled by day-off boozers
politicians palely bang the drum:
we must remember those who stuffed the Germans,
whose tragic deaths kept Britain Great.
What blousy things to die for;
flags and sunshine, lips and lager.

In the cool abbey
where stones shine like water
I sit beside an unwreathed grave.
'To the Gods, the Shades, Flavinius,
a horse soldier of the Cavalry Regiment of Petriana,
Standard Bearer of the Troop of Candidus,
25 years of age, having served 7 years in the army,
is here laid, for the Glory of Rome.'

Reflections from a bonefield
on this most glorious day.
The greatest tragedy of the dead,
the bastards left to talk for them.

A Leaving

Branches cup their shreds of leaves,
there is an ancient wall translated into moss
and two glens,
one chipped into the stone blue sky
and sloping east to a dwam* of light
like water,
the other eery, unbroken on the loch,
though in the wind the mountains shudder down,
even to my shoes.

In such times
it is more difficult to see
the start and end of things,
which is as well.
This morning I am leaving her on Mull,
as I have done before,
only this time she is scattered through
the trees and the soil and the somersaulting water
so from now on, no matter the weather,
the island will speak in only one
gentle voice.

* dwam: *a confusing blur.*

Dear Sammy

There are things here that you would know
and some that would make you gasp.
The new moon's here, breathing on the grass
and sharp tongues of water glow
in the hills. Summer's nearly past.
Along the river, right down the glen,
the trees are fiery brown again.

But the people here you wouldn't understand.
I don't know where they're from. Lapland,
or Mars I sometimes think. There's a man
here who thinks that Jimmy Shand
is an eastern town, on some caravan
route from China, and Burns Night was banned
for being racist, or some such word.
They flew kites instead, and ate smörgåsbord.

They walk about in feathers
like apaches. Mind you, they're clever:
they've a shop selling leather,
and little glass elves.
They sell them to tourists. Folk like themselves.
But at least they're of Scottish blood, Sammy,
their name's on the door, it says Macrami.

It sounds a long way, England
but I suppose it's not so far.
Sometimes I can't stand
to think of how things are.
Oh, you'd have laughed —
they had a feast for Beltane night
with dancing and mead on draught,
sacrifice and other rites.
It was the wrongs of winter we had to celebrate,

Sammy; that made you emigrate.
The Macramis play the didgeridoo.
Are there many hills near Crewe?

On the Retirement of Mr. D. Douglas

Atque inter silvas Academi quaerere verum
as the dead teachers of a dead culture would say.
No more wine dark seas and winged words,
only the chocolate flavoured Nith
and chip papers mimicking.
Seek truth in the groves of Academe;
but there's a notion now
that you can teach
without telling the truth,
without *speaking* even.
Remember the story of the man
who, talking gently and firmly,
taught gulls to sing like larks?
Mutato nomine de te fabulo narratur.

Nebelgard Girl

I shone the iron wheels of her cart
as she bathed in the mere
with long necked birds.

My sisters necklaced me with samphire,
twisted tansy in my hair.
They sighed when they saw my breasts
just budded, but

my skin will not be jowled or scarred.
Look at me as I leave my hearth,
smell the broom on my breath,
I will be the mother

no man has forced.
Mark it! When I am gone
flowers will seep through the earth like milk.

Graeco-Roman Culture

1.
The Acropolis, Lyndos.
Below, blue spirals between stalks of rock
and beyond, to backs of islands
inching above the lip of distance like whales.
What angles,
what spinning light to burn dreams on stone.
The men who built this dizziness
had eyes lidless, like the sun.

2.
Hardknott Pass,
quarters carved from guts of granite,
grey slate and scrim, blown like sand.
Above, clouds knot like rope,
fill the gaps between broken shafts of mountain.
These little hard men,
leaving their slough of monuments,
built no temples.
They dreamed
of anoraks.

Tucker, as Always

Three old heids, hands held up
but not in surrender.
Tucker's one:
Tucker round as a barrel,
voice like gravel,
Tucker of the iron bicycle,
of the mower and the roller,
Tucker who flattened fields
for summer children sprouted and dispersed.
"Cairo, Alexandria, Tel Aviv, Dumfries ...
all mine" he says in his most corrugated tone.
"Tucker, look" says his pal,
pushing a rum winking like a ruby,
"that's your's too".
Tucker recalls what is his,
what was his,
the infant skies,
the desert harsh as longing,
his life a legend in miniatures.
"I'll take it", he says,
"as always".

Saturday 21st May

Leaving Dundee;
crows dummy run at fence posts,
the fields stretching flat as you can imagine
to the shapes of hills.
Little chimneys peep out, coy in trees,
and horses bend their heads.
Opposite, sombre suited,
some apparatchiks discuss the death of John Smith.
The emotion in Scotland, they say,
it is the mark of the man.
Perhaps, though it is more than that, and less.
Today, in the graveyard of Kings,
they are burying the perfect head of state for us,
unburdened by the inconvenience of public office,
the leader who never was,
of a country that is,
and isn't.

The X Files: Bonnybridge, October '95

Lorrayne
before you hit me with that object
shaped like a toblerone
let me explain.
We only went for a half pint and a whisky
then set off home but somehow
lost two hours on a thirty minute journey.
My mind's a blank
but Brian clearly saw
Aliens with black eyes and no lips
leading us onto a kind of craft.
I tried to lash out, explain that I was late,
but they used some kind of numbing ray on me:
it put me in this state.
Lorrayne, don't you see what it explains?
All the times I crawled home with odd abrasions.
Put that down Lorrayne,
don't you see I *have* to go again,
for the sake of future generations?

What You Feel Before You Get Eaten by a Bear

July,
the moon high above rags of cloud.
I was swinging a bag,
some crushed rubbish ready for the skip,
and I was thinking,
even in those mountains with the smell
of burnt wood and flowers,
about Rangers, how much I hated them,
and whether, back at the bar,
they would think my drink was finished
and take it away,
when suddenly I saw a bear,
standing two, three feet above me,
mouth shining,
eyes rolling like marbles,
a Brown Bear, a Carpathian Bear,
the type that follows Romanians home
as a matter of course and eats them.
And in that calm when the nerves,
mugged by alcohol, are like ice,
there was a moment when I felt
I suppose like those boys in Toubacanti,
one moment embarking at Leith among the
gulls and smell of fish
the next dodging with naked Indians
between the red legged mangroves
swiping at Conquistadors,
there was a moment,
at the teeth of it,
when I felt
Scottish.

Hans from Wuppertal

Hans from Wuppertal they called him,
in the bare-bulb nights in camp,
Hans who tells stories.
Long into the evenings
with ice patterning on windows
he would spin them tales
of the forests of Thuringia,
dark tales for the dark.
Hans from Wuppertal, they would say,
Hans the liar.
After the war, in Brooke Street,
in his little room filled with stamps,
he would tell stories too,
about flying planes in the war,
planes with no propellors.
Oh Aye, we'd say, Hans the Liar.
After he died, his sister,
whose letters he had returned unopened,
told us how he was the Reich's favourite Test Pilot,
aide de camp to Goering,
Hans, it turned out, from Wannsee.

Reflections on the Aphrodite of Rhodes

Thoughtful tourist,
musing on the transience of grandeur, pause.
Forget the swelling of my breast,
the thighs' white gloss,
the impish angle of my chin,
and look, as I hold it out, at my hair!
Knots of string,
and no wonder;
it's hard to keep a coiffeur intact
two thousand years below a tobacconist's.
I used to look quite good, in fact,
like that bitch Tiramanitis,
all curls and clasps and look at the smile.
Now I'm only fit for this glass case,
the wanton part of a before and after piece
on Hellenistic Style.

History at Knossos

History is the thing that translates cowpats
into frescoes of rent boys and bimbo snake goddesses.
It's the thing that turns quarries into colonnades
guarded by men in underpants from C and A's.
History is maladjusted Victorians
thinking their wives were Helen,
their mothers Pasiphak,
and their penises the source of centipedes and scorpions.
History is that Spanish guide with a parasol
stamping near the site of the first flushing toilet,
shouting *Aqui! Aqui!*
Here sat King Minos!

The Stone Princess

In a landscape of mud
past sentry posts of gutted fridge
sandstone rises
dead, like a city from the sea.
Water from lintels,
and shattered frets of window,
pools in her tomb.
Once prettily carved and psalmed over,
she is smooth as a fish,
her head a grape,
her body tapering to amputated toes.
Someone has drawn teats and eyes;
it doesn't shock.
They are priestesses these youths
chalking ghosts on stone.
They sit and drink here,
touch her belly for luck,
fuck her.
She has not eroded,
just lost her Anglo-Norman angles on life.

Vlad the Inhaler

Cortes Des Arges.
A thousand steps cut in yellow rock.
We climb through scents, and sunlight
darting between the lips of trees.
Above us the sky seems pinned by birch stacks.
Sometimes, at a dog-leg,
the light spins, crescents dizzily down,
and the ground is lost, dissolved.
Only the climb remains,
the drum of breath,
and the scream of birds.
At the first hint of wall
a soldier appears from loops of shadow.
He wants cigarettes,
settles for a wrist band for his girl.
The Dragon's Castle he says,
I guard it. I keep it safe.
He waves his rifle like a man
who has been too long in the woods,
and we pass, emerging at a pinnacle
to the expected haemorrhage of light.

Targets

I have this picture,
set against the penetrating greens
that memory ignites;
my dog running towards me
six inches above the Birks of Aberfeldy,
the berk of Aberfeldy,
rotor ears and tail
and tongue like a red banner,
beating the air,
advancing frame by frame
his bullet head cocked
at the centre of the lens,
daring my attention to wander off line,
to forces more fatal than gravity.

Aine

There's a dazzling slick of light on the water
as if some unlagged pipe has burst
and the sun is bubbling out.
It's nearly November
but Summer is hanging over Oban
like a comic ending the season on a private joke.
Trippers swelter on the Esplanade
in tweeds and cable stitching,
shake their heads,
wonder if David Icke wasn't right about the weather
and if the water round Kerrera — deepest turquoise —
isn't proof of it.
But if they looked over their papers at the right moment,
if they'd drunk the right amount of Bruachladich,
if their grannies had once been snogged
by the wild west wind,
they might just see the cause,
strolling in that crook of tar
between the Dog Rock and Dunollie,
miracles in her canvas bag
and fire, summoned through the wands of masts,
burning in her hair.

Address to a Galway Pen

A poem was on my neck like a bat,
but in the barnyard of William Street
it squirmed away.
Now, in the boozy light,
you glint, not nicely.

Oh don't leave me like the others,
in Ladbrokes, or a warm pub,
or in some cafe folded to the breast of a crossword,
don't get lost in my lining and burst,
or desert me for a postcard writer;
such work is not for you,
your sleek lines gleam with publight,
stars ripple in your length,
there is magic in you.

You could carve me metaphors
that would get my work snapped up,
praised by eggheads,
printed in anthologies,
or listen, one night
with the moon swimming through glass,
perhaps at a table like this
beaten down by elbows,
haunted by beer,
you could write

and what you write
might pierce the heart of the paper
like a sharpened stick
and the need to break the skin
would bleed, at last, away.

Easdale

A jetty, and stumps of cottages
in the wind, doors
gaping like mouths.

On one window, a shred of curtain
is still stuck on the glass. Smudged blue,
like babies' eyes, it belies the museum
calm, speaks of children
nursed here, not imported half made
from Guildford.

Across the Sound a coach spills
its tourists on the Arts
and Crafts. They are searching for the
spirit of Highlands, long gone,
like the miners, like the tide,
quiet as ledgers.

Getting too Late for Football

Clouds shoulder the moon
and the sky is bruising
scarlet and navy blue.
The town, tiny in the palm of hills,
thins to silhouette,
the broken fingers of the trees,
the spires, the stubs of houses,
all blending to an aromatic
childhood chocolate brown
with me in the middle
vanishing like the dot on a TV screen —
a diminution signifying
more this time than a memory of bedtime —
and it's only the nagging cold,
the dull gleam of the football
and Andy calling from the
elbow of a goalpost for one last kick
that remind me
there are things still to do
and a route to try and find
through the dark.

Blethers*

For two nights
I've teetered on this page
high above bronchial trucks
and winking snugs.
I've doodled and dribbled
an incontinent love
and out of it came a poem,
a piece of literary machismo,
that was going to leave you breathless.
My, you would gasp in awe,
that fairly sums it up.
What rot.

You have given me your heart.
I see it in your worried eyes,
in the slow detonation of your smile.
I see it even here
in the soot and stones,
through gangling miles of cloud and sea.
What's a poem compared with that?
Blethers.

* Blethers: *spoken rubbish.*

On the Hoof

I'm leaving Stranraer, replete,
the ribs of my last meal rattling at my feet.
Outside the bus there are layers of light,
fields are salt white,
the sea is dark as caramel.
A few trees dip tall
heads like parasols high
in a cocktail of clouds and streaky sky.

The girl opposite, nibbling a roll,
has hair that gleams in little seams like coal
as she bends down.
Her eyes are warm, her skin toast brown,
and I am reminded that all in all
there is enough in the south west
for everyone to digest;
the poet and the cannibal.

Obersalzberg

Looking down, the bathers
are little spits of meat
in the furnace of the day,
their umbrellas spreading like a rash.

Above, trees jab at the skin of the sky,
and the road curls away like smoke,
the forest drumming at our heels,
the crickets rattling,
birds exploding through the grass like shot.

Greens dilute. Trees wither.
We trudge on, past a last bleached Calvary,
to where the mountain wriggles in the saw teeth of the sun
and a song beyond notation scalds our hearts.

Sports Day

July.
The sun, dripping honey-tongued,
dapples brown-legged girls;
peels back starker shades of
green and white.

Through slatted eyes
runners swim in fog, slower,
though cries, far off, electric,
tell of records broken.
Melted, more like.

Minutes hiss and sink like embers.
Drifting,
we are pale, translucent.
Beached, the runners
fade to distant dreams of light.

Louisiana Train

Funnelling through the night,
suddenly the lights shut off.
I lost sight of my maps, my beer,
the old lady with the rings,
the black eyed girl sad I was so ugly,
and instead the nearest thing
was a horizon burning with orange
and a thumbnail line of hills
bending round the moon,
and it was suddenly like Falkirk,
Falkirk for fuck's sake,
coming to Falkirk on a Saturday in winter
with the results on the teleprinter
and you in that green euphemism of a car,
that excuse for a birl* against the odds,
ticking in the car park like a bomb.
Then the lights came back
too late
and the train surged on into the body of the night
with me sticking in its throat.

* birl: *an adventure.*

Letter from the 24th Congress of the Communist Party

(inspired by photographs of the event)

Dear Joe,
Sorry you couldn't be here,
you really missed yourself.
Krupskaya brought a quiche
but the fun really started when Bukharin
told the joke about the dyslexic deviant functionalists
and when Felix Dzerhinsky got his cock out,
turned his pockets inside out
and pretended to be Babar,
I thought I'd die.
Who said the inevitable victory of the Proletariat
was bound to be joyless?
Love Vlad.

History

The last whaler lives
in a cottage with black sills
sunk like a bad tooth in Henry Street.
The other houses gleam in a practised smile
that brings tourists to one side,
and artists to a salon on the other.
The street no longer stinks of blood
but peppermint.

The Whaler has a wicker chair
and a bottle of beer
stashed below.
Fuck youse he shouts at the trippers,
at the bohemians fleeing with their paints,
fuck youse all
and he grins the wet width of his gums.

In the craftshop
among the pictures of local characters
there are no entries
for the year our man was born,
on the beach, they say,
in the shape of a dog.
After all, is it the kind of thing
you want to hear on your holiday,
a pensioner urging you to abandon
the Museum of Automata,
to go instead and fuck yourself?

They are waiting, waiting,
for an incident serious enough
to have him removed,
strangled in his bed by a hit-man
from the National Trust
and replaced, no fuss,
with a hologram or a polystyrene head
that says

Hello Boys and Girls
come in and see my life:
it was hard but we had fringe religions
and folk music,
peppermint and little crosses made from jet,
some of which are on sale inside
for as little as three quid,
for history surely

a small price to pay.

At the Swings

Puddles,
and bracelets of scuffed bloom.
The wet trees butt water
and the river noses past the bridge,
the arches stubbled with moss,
to where reeds swim with sandstone
in a black mirage
and only the punctuation of swans,
bent like question marks,
dazzle.

He swings,
his bright red shoes a challenge
to the consensus of cloud and rooftiles,
the wash of grey and green.
He stretches out his hands,
palm outwards,
"I can let go, and hold onto nothing."

He's kept me moored like a full stop
on this page
that he'll desert one day
without a thought.
There's colour in the world,
a dazzle of colour,
but where could I go to see
such a brush stroke,
bold against the sky?
I could let go,
but I would hold onto nothing.

Surprise Attacks

I hear the sound of a boy
waiting to be ambushed
by his father,
that carpet of smells and roars
like a bear, all hugs and stubble.
Each step breaks on the stairs like ice
and it precedes him, this excitement,
like a shadow mad and off its moorings.
Oh should we not weep
for the ghosts of undiluted joy
and the years I cannot wish for him
but he is eager, all fists, for.

It is a long minute.
He is stopped, poised on one leg
like a crane.
Perhaps he will be a dancer
or a poet
it doesn't matter.
Whether he requires it for his art or not
he will be ambushed by his father,
from the tops of trees
the tips of pencils
the precipitation of sleep
he will be ambushed by his father,
when he is old and threadbare
and sick of such surprises,
even then
he will be ambushed by his father.

Bus Station

All the stances
like sad banners,
like sunken stones.
People are drawn and repelled by them,
these long doors opening and closing,
most knowing it's the same.
Children play at their feet,
and long concrete horizons balloon away.
The engines fire,
purple smoke billowing like unanswered rage,
and that's how they leave,
the children winding after them
like torn flags.

The Zoo

A speckled gorge of sky and rain drumming.
The sun parts sheaves of cloud
with wide white palms.
There's a torrent of children
beating down the grass,
breaking against the steep sides
of ice cream vans,
scattering like deer at the sight of Keepers,
snooping parents or Rockhoppers
swimming for their skin.

Andrew's in the middle,
trailing his knuckles along the ground,
telling parrots to shut up,
howling like a timberwolf,
trampling his zooburger,
rolling eyes at the Marmosets.
As I drag him screaming past
the Vietnamese Pot Bellied Pigs
they draw genteely back.
It seems that plain good manners
got these beasts in stir.

Outside the gates, in the hard heat
of the evening, buses swarm
and hoot and beat away toward the town.
The animals yawn like old lags
and the kids are leaving.
They shouldn't cry.
This brush with sad old nature's
just a taste:
the jungle's nearer than they think.

Rumours

Sitting on a knoll
as the fields lap at us,
unbroken green shuddering like a swell.
"When are you going to war?"
asks Andrew casually,
"will you get me caps?"

I explain I will only fight Martians,
some cock eyed nonsense
he doesn't hear.
He's squinting at the horizon,
watching the invasion of the afternoon,
the fuse of light burning.
Somewhere, stubble is smoking.

"Forget the caps" I whisper,
as we wade through grass,
and he's crying
when the sun drops behind hills
like blood.

Angles

Three window panes,
a triptych of smithereens,
of sun on water,
gulls tight-roping on mastheads,
hills groggy with sandstone
gawping at the sea,
and the sound of Kerrera
careering away like a big laddie
to butt the Hebrides.

Nearer, through the third pane,
a muddle of shadow and light,
the room bounced through a riot of glass
onto a wall outside.
No tourists look in here,
only I can detect an infinity of you,
your smile blazing to pinprick size,
to tickle dimensions beyond the glamour
of eyeshot.

Shug, Alex, Jock, Willie ...

Hang about my head like shoplifters.
I have to follow them,
escort them firmly from my mind.
If I relax they'll have my imagination up their jouks*
in a jiffy and be running down the road.

Most of the time they're safe on Kodachrome,
prison striped with sunlight,
or caught rat-eyed in cellar bars
but sometimes in my dreams they visit me.
Draped in woolly blankets
they ask formal questions about the price of fish,
boast of slippery girls
or the songs they've sung with whales.

They shake their arm at me
and wail about the folk who've pilfered their identities,
use their names to prop up bills
and business cards
and the little things they send you
when your books are overdue.

What do you want, I ask of them.
You, they say.
You,
and our time again.

* jouks: *jumpers.*

Lynn Wilson Says a Prayer for Robert Burns

In St. Michael's they are commemorating Burns.
The sun fires corkscrews of dust
as cameramen tussle
and the static screams.

A Minister directs the telescopic lens
to the pew where Jean and Robert sat.
The man himself is gone.
He will be reconstituted later, like a burger,
from scrapings on the Studio floor,
but now ...

Behind me,
in an old blend of wood
and light thrown through green windows,
a young girl sits in prayer.
Her head is bent. Her hair is like a flame.

Beauty,
and bedlam.

A commemoration after all.

The Little Summer of San Demetrios

(God turned nature on its end for St. Demetrius when the friar prayed for
good weather so that he might cross the winter sea, go home to his
manuscripts and sheep.)

In the little summer of San Demetrios
sun ignites shale,
waterfalls drop like dull fire,
embers toppling at the end of a blaze.
We climb through light
to the coolness of riverpools.
Below, cars blow along the road like dust.

Hours pass.
In the little summer of San Demetrios
your lips are like fruit
but your eyes are rapt,
following the curve of hills,
the road that sloughs to Moffat,
the way back.
Come on, I say, *let's go on*,
the little summer of San Demetrios is for travellers.

Night is coming,
wind doubles the grass.
It is the way; the eye is closing.
It is time for going home, you say,
the little summer of San Demetrios.
Clouds gather, slowly join.
There will be such darkness
and for the lost, rain.

The Cargo of the 'Hopeful Binning of Bo'ness', Bound for the Darien Peninsula, 1699

140 periwigs
26 camel coats
210 Broons' Books (Large print edition)
3 Gross string vests (should have been 3 gross string vests?)
25,000 Jean Redpath CDs
184 bundles of kindling
406 tea towels
1 accordian
120 copies of 'Trainspotting' by Irvine Welsh (Dutch language version)
4 brillo pads
1 Lena Martell Old Rugged Cross Karaoke Video
4,020 sets of dominoes
and
some loose change.

As We Go Home

Rain grazes the road,
cuts its way to the valley
where Dumfries is lighting up
like an old man,
in coughs and starts.
We pass a tree,
a bag spreadeagled in the branches,
a sign nailed to its chin,
Fear Ye the Lord.

Yesterday the trees were like sails
on the Ramblas
and the sun too was silk
and yes there were plastic bags
but not bayonneted like this one,
empty ribs swinging on a gibbet,
half the logo gone,
HAD ...
Haddows,
or Hades.

Fear ye the Lord
and the clouds gathering
as we go home.

In Search of Leanne

Remember? She was the one
whispering in my ear on the West Coast Line,
delivering me, on the same plate,
visions of Winter and Spring?
She was the one that shook the flowers,
parted the clouds to show
the slow and splintering world.
Where is she?
I thought she lived for my visits,
spent the times between growing mushrooms,
or lightening the dawn around Barrhead.
I hope she's not defected:
Her intercession would win Pete Fortune
the Scottish Book Award that I deserve,
and what would become of her?
He would use her endlessly.
Unlike me,
her chaste lover.
I used to brush her lips,
there, like that,
a very small kiss,
enough,
for a poem to come.

Hole in the Wa' — April '96

Four o'clock.
Outside, kids rush back from school
and arrowing geese scorn thermals
home in a blur of blue
but here in a light like an Old Master's,
scuffed by years or boots,
they are standing,
elbows hooked like batwings on the bar,
Tucker,
George,
the Major,
Annie,
turning noses into beer,
beer into spit,
life into shadows,
a day into dreaming.

So George, scarlet faced,
paces the bar like a poop deck
while the Major sways in his wake
and Hammie screams like a mandril
and Willie Gail sings,
his finger in the sticky air
scratching time to whole forgotten words

and Tucker, bent legs bowed,
will tell you of his day,
the crowd not ba' heids in newsreel brown
but folk glorious in maroon,
the sun full on their faces, cheering
as Tucker cuts, in brilliant green,
his piece of ancient history

and the man with the hat
shows snaps of his grandson
who is mostly seven
and sometimes called Steven
but who always calls him Poppa,
not the man with the plastic bag
whose forehead kisses the bar,
but Poppa.

And so it is,
and time never passes here,
no-one dies,
but is replaced

and time never passes here,
only clocks move dark hands
round and round,
like other people's lives.

Saturday Afternoon in the Grotto

Santa's in Sauchiehall Street.
There's a file of cheery white faced boys
with convict cuts and little oval heads like eggs
and bright red freckles,
as if someone had stood at the front of the queue
with a paintbrush, flicking it.

Their Dads, more used to snug bars than grottos,
are wheezing and stamping with the cold,
playfully cuffing ears,
sharing in the seasonal enthusiasm for chimneys
by smoking like them.
The result is a surreal and Scottish kind
of Christmas ambience

with rubber reindeer lurching drunkenly
through the fog
and tattooed men crunching, blind, through
polyester snow, scything down the penguins
and eyeing up the elf who's taking photographs:
give her a ride in my sleigh anyday.

It's happy enough
but I am a father of a more modern calibre
so I was disappointed to see Andrew vault
like a paratrooper from Santa's knee,
pick a handgun from the box
and cock it jauntily at the girl behind the polaroid
as if to say:
*not much call for the Spyrographs this afternoon
is there Doll?*

Happy New Year

Dumfries: mid-day.
When I lift the blind the room gets darker.
Outside, little trees skinned to a T-Shirt of bark gather
like casuals, chatter in the wind.
In the background, caged Christmas trees glimmer.
This is Scotland, January 3rd.
It looks like a landscape stricken by germ warfare,
stripped of warmth, colour,
any signs that in the rest of the world pass for life.
Mid-day, mid-night:
In the distance two men in anoraks converge,
to strangle each other.